This Book Belongs To:

____

BY
Home Planners And
Journals
To help you organize your life

www.ingramcontent.com/pod-product-compliance
Lightning Source LLC
Chambersburg PA
CBHW071221240726

48654CB00009B/870